CROCK

ARE THOSE YOUR GOOD PANTS?

by

Bill Rechin and Don Wilder

D0681028

FAWCETT GOLD MEDAL • NEW YORK

ARE THOSE YOUR GOOD PANTS?

Published by Fawcett Gold Medal Books, a unit of CBS
Publications, the Consumer Publishing Division of CBS Inc.,
by special arrangement with Field Newspaper Syndicate.

ISBN: 0-449-14390-2

Printed in the United States of America

First Fawcett Gold Medal printing: February 1981

10   9   8   7   6   5   4   3   2   1

GASP!..... SIR, I AIN'T HAD A DRINK OF WATER IN TWO YEARS ....CHOKE.....WHEEZE... ...COULD YOU SPARE A DROP?

Bill Rechin

EVERY TIME I TURN AROUND, IT'S "GIMME, GIMME, GIMME!"

THE ALMANAC SAYS IT'S GONNA BE A LONG, COLD WINTER.
I DON'T BELIEVE THAT JUNK
WOULD MY FURRY TOENAILS LIE TO ME?

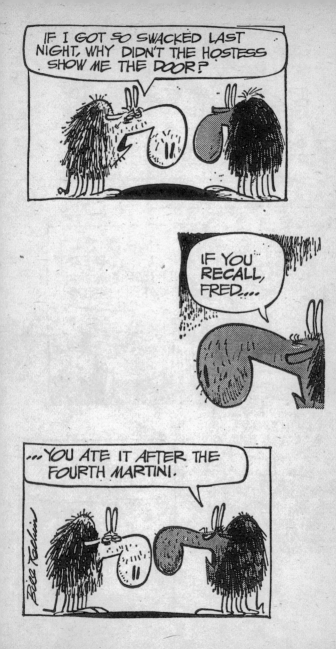

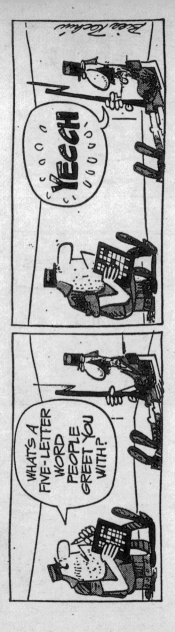

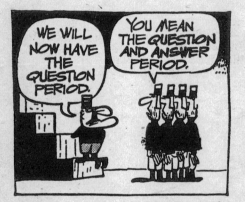

SIR, THE MEN ARE RIOTING, THE AMMO DUMP IS ON FIRE, AND OUTPOST FIVE IS UNDER ATTACK...
...WHAT'S YOUR SOLUTION?
Bill Rechin
LAST SEASON KEEPING MY HEAD DOWN ON MY FOLLOW-THROUGH DID THE TRICK.
TAP

YOU GOT A LETTER FROM THE LAKERIDGE BEGONIA CLUB.

...THEY ACCEPTED YOUR OFFER TO DECORATE THE FORT

YOU KNOW CROCK HATES FLOWERS.

WELL, I HAPPEN TO LIKE BEGONIAS

...NOT AFTER YOU EAT THE FIRST TWO HUNDRED

6.7

Bill Rechin

I HEAR YOU WANT TO JOIN THE LEGION

...IT'S A GREAT LIFE... LOOK WHAT IT'S DONE FOR ME

DON'T WORRY... WE'LL GET YOU THE BEST DOCTORS MONEY CAN BUY.